ABDO Publishing Company

BUGS!
Flies

Kristin Petrie

visit us at
www.abdopublishing.com

Published by ABDO Publishing Company, 8000 West 78th Street, Edina, Minnesota 55439.

Printed in the United States.

Cover Photo: iStockphoto
Interior Photos: Alamy p. 24; Andy Williams/CritterZone.com p. 21; Corbis p. 23;
    Getty Images pp. 11, 12–13, 27; iStockphoto p. 1; Joseph Berger/Bugwood.org pp. 9, 28;
    Peter Ambruzs/CritterZone.com p. 15; Peter Arnold pp. 19, 22, 25; Photo Researchers p. 29;
    Sturgis McKeever/Bugwood.org pp. 5, 17; Whitney Cranshaw/Bugwood.org p. 16;
    William Vann/edupic.net p. 7

Series Coordinator: BreAnn Rumsch
Editors: Megan M. Gunderson, BreAnn Rumsch
Art Direction & Cover Design: Neil Klinepier

Library of Congress Cataloging-in-Publication Data

Petrie, Kristin, 1970-
 Flies / Kristin Petrie.
    p. cm. -- (Bugs!)
 Includes index.
 ISBN 978-1-60453-068-1
 1. Flies--Juvenile literature. I. Title.

QL533.2.P48 2008
595.77--dc22
                                2008004791

Contents

Fascinating Flies

What is black, bright green, or metallic blue? It also has hair, wings, and a strawlike mouth. Bulging eyes cover most of its head. Last, this creature seems to love you and your food. Give up? It's a fly!

The flies you encounter can be very pesky. Some flies are merely annoying. They buzz around slowly and clumsily. They bump right into windows, walls, and your face. Others may cause more serious problems. These flies are quick as lightning. They bite you again and again, zipping out of your reach each time.

Most of us only want to know one thing about flies. That is how to get rid of them. In fact, the U.S. government spends millions of dollars each year to limit the fly population.

Still, flies are fascinating creatures. They have adapted to many ways of life. It seems they are here to stay! Keep reading to discover something about flies you may not have known before.

Most flies have the large eyes you may already be familiar with.
These eyes help them pilot their way through the air.

What Are They?

Flies belong to the class Insecta. Within this class, they belong to the order Diptera. This name comes from Greek words meaning "two wings." The order Diptera is divided into many families. Among these families, there are more than 120,000 fly species.

Each species of fly has a two-word name called a binomial. A binomial combines the genus with a descriptive name, or epithet. For example, a bluebottle fly's binomial is *Calliphora vomitoria*.

The word *fly* is part of the common names of many insects. Yet, insects such as butterflies and dragonflies are not true flies. To add to the confusion, not all dipterans have the word *fly* in their common names. For example, did you know that mosquitoes and gnats are flies?

How do you tell a true fly from a false one? True flies have two wings instead of four! This makes the ordinary fly seem a little more interesting. Before you squash that bug, you may want to get a closer look. Can you tell whether it is really a fly?

Flies come in many shapes and sizes. Some are thick and round. Others are skinny and long-legged, such as this crane fly.

THAT'S CLASSIFIED!

Scientists use a method called scientific classification to sort the world's living organisms into groups. Eight groups make up the basic classification system. In descending order, they are domain, kingdom, phylum, class, order, family, genus, and species.

The phrase "Dear King Philip, come out for goodness' sake!" may help you remember this order. The first letter of each word is a clue for each group.

Domain is the most basic group. Species is the most specific group. Members of a species share common characteristics. Yet, they are different from all other living things in at least one way.

Body Parts

What would you do if a black, hairy blob landed on your hamburger? Chances are, that bug is a fly. Let's take a closer look to identify some of its features.

Not all flies are black blobs. These bugs range in color. Some fly species are bright green or metallic blue. Others are multicolored. They may have stripes like a bumblebee or spots like a ladybug.

Flies also range in size. Midges are as small as a pinhead. Due to their tiny size, they are also known as no-see-ums. The largest fly species is the robber fly. These flying monsters can grow to almost three inches (7 cm) long. Imagine that landing on your lunch!

Fly bodies are covered with hairs and **spines** that have a very cool job. These hairs and spines sense vibrations and changes in air movement. No wonder flies are so hard to swat! When you move toward one, the air in front of you hits the fly first. This tells the fly to scram!

Because of their coloring, blowflies are often called bluebottles or greenbottles. Whatever their color, all flies are hairy bugs!

A fly's body has three **segments**. These are the head, the thorax, and the abdomen. The head features antennae, eyes, and a mouth. A fly uses its antennae to smell food and feel changes in air movement. Some fly species have antennae that are short and pointed like horns. Others have antennae that are long and feathery.

Fly mouths also come in different styles. Each fly's mouthparts include palpi and a proboscis. Palpi are feelers that can touch and examine foods.

Some species have a bladelike proboscis. The hard tip pierces food like a tiny knife. Then, a strawlike groove is used for sucking up liquid foods such as blood. Other species have a softer proboscis. At the tip, soft and spongy labella soak up liquid foods.

The fly's compound eyes dominate its head. Each bulging eyeball is composed of thousands of tiny lenses. These lenses work together to detect light, shapes, and movement. They can also see in all directions at once. This is another reason why flies are so hard to catch!

Houseflies have spongelike mouthparts. Other flies that have similar mouthparts include fruit flies and blowflies.

Beyond the fly's head is its thorax. Powerful muscles in this middle **segment** control the fly's legs and wings. The fly has six long, jointed legs. Sensory hairs cover each one. The legs are used for landing, walking, and holding prey.

Each leg ends in a clawed foot. Many flies also have sticky pads on their feet. These help the fly grasp objects and walk upside down. The pads also allow the fly to taste what it has landed on!

The fly's two wings are made of a tough material called chitin. Veins running through the wings make interesting patterns. They are used to help identify individual species. The veins also supply blood, making the wings stiff and strong.

Behind the veined wings lie two stubs. These undeveloped wings are called halteres. Only true flies have halteres. They balance the fly while it is in the air, even when flying backward!

WING

The abdomen is the third and last **segment** of the fly's body. Many fly species have what looks like a waist between the thorax and the abdomen. Some flies have long, slender abdomens. Others have short, round abdomens. These features help **entomologists** identify fly species.

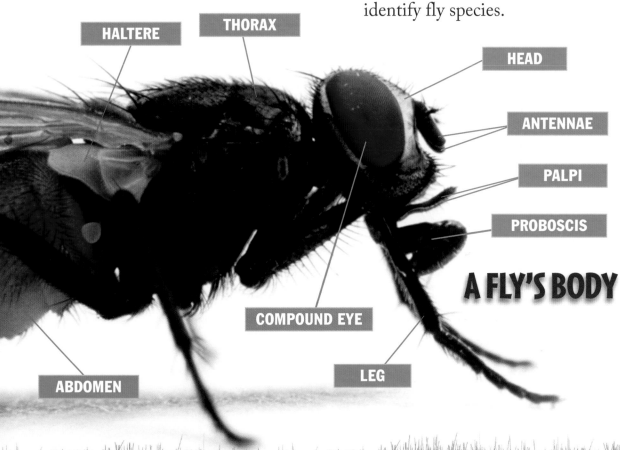

HALTERE

THORAX

HEAD

ANTENNAE

PALPI

PROBOSCIS

A FLY'S BODY

COMPOUND EYE

LEG

ABDOMEN

The Inside Story

Inside a fly, several systems work together to keep its body moving. Like most insects, a fly's heart is a simple, long tube. The heart carries blood from one end of the fly's body to the other. Fly blood is called hemolymph. It flows freely throughout the fly's body. This is called an open circulatory system.

A fly's respiratory system begins with holes called spiracles. The thorax has two pairs of spiracles. There are eight more on the abdomen. Oxygen enters the fly's body through these holes. Then, a series of tubes called tracheae deliver the air throughout the fly's body.

A simple brain and a **nerve** cord make up a fly's nervous system. The brain consists of clusters of nerves called ganglia. Ganglia in the thorax and the abdomen connect to the brain by the nerve cord. Nerves extend from the cord through the fly's body. These nerves help control the fly's movements and **organs**.

A mosquito's abdomen swells as it feeds on blood. Nerves in its abdomen tell it when to stop eating. Otherwise, the mosquito would feed until its body burst.

Transformation

A fly's life cycle is called complete **metamorphosis**. There are four stages in this type of life cycle. They are egg, larva, pupa, and adult. Some fly species complete the entire life cycle in several weeks. Other species take a full year to reach adulthood.

To begin the life cycle, a male and female fly must mate. The flies may have attracted one another through **pheromones**. Or, they may have developed into adults at the same place. After mating, females begin producing **fertilized** eggs.

Some fly species produce hundreds of eggs. Others make just a few. Not all fly species handle their eggs the same way. Some females keep their eggs within their bodies. Others lay their eggs through an **organ** called an ovipositor. Most mothers lay their eggs on or inside their favorite food source.

Mating often begins with an act of courtship. This may include a dance performed by the male for the female. It may also include males competing for a female.

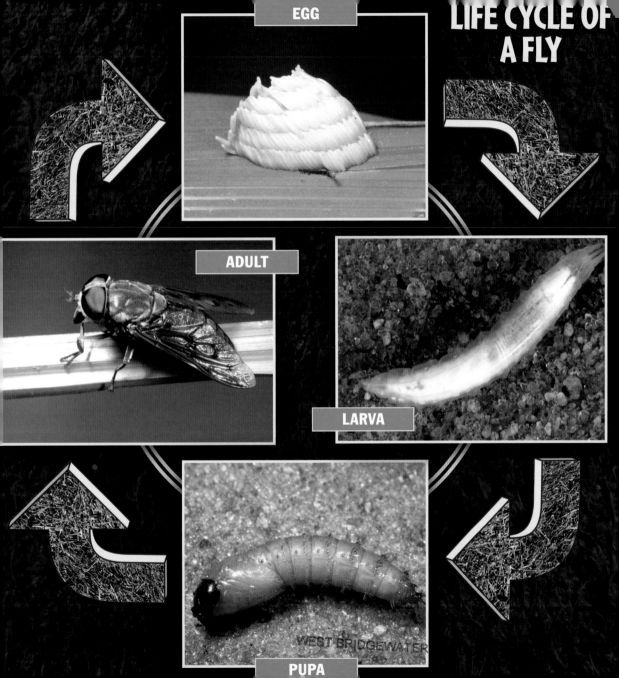

Soon, the eggs hatch into larvae. Larvae of common flies, such as houseflies, are also called maggots. They look like small, white, headless worms. Maggots are often found in rotting food and animal waste.

Since the larvae have been carefully placed at their food source, they immediately start to eat. Larvae eat and eat until they grow out of their skin. This is called molting. Fly larvae molt several times. The final molt leads the larvae to the next stage in their life cycle.

The pupal stage begins when the skin around the larvae hardens. This hardened skin resembles a cocoon. At first, the pupal cases are creamy white. As the young flies age, the cases turn a darker brown color.

Inside, the pupae stay very still to conserve their energy. Soon, an amazing change takes place. The wormy larvae that went into the pupal cases transform into adult flies.

When the transformation is complete, adult flies pop out of the pupal cases. Their wings are fully formed and quickly harden. They can fly soon after the pupal cases break. This allows adult flies to get right to work. Their job is to find food and a mate.

WATER BABIES

Unlike other fly species, most mosquitoes lay their eggs in water. Ponds and swamps are commonly used.

Mosquito larvae look much different from other fly species. These larvae have short, tubular bodies and hairy heads. They hang just beneath the water's surface and breathe through air tubes that reach above the water. Mosquito larvae are often called wrigglers. This is because they wriggle to catch their floating dinner.

Mosquito pupae are similar to other fly species. However, they can swim! Their shape allows them to roll and tumble in the water. So, they are called tumblers. After several days, they emerge above water as adults and fly away.

Fly Homes

It's true that flies hang out in many of the places you go. They love to buzz around your house, yard, bus, and school. In fact, flies can survive almost anywhere, from deserts to the Arctic Circle.

Yet, flies love to live in warm places most of all. Tropical areas such as rain forests are loaded with flies. There, they feast on tons of plant and animal food sources. Plentiful sources of water and moisture quench their thirst. And, warm weather promotes rapid growth.

Obviously, not all flies live in tropical areas. For example, fruit flies live on fruit, fruit trees, and other plants. Mosquitoes and blackflies live near water. And, the famous housefly lives in houses and other buildings around the world.

Robber flies prefer dry, sandy, open areas where they can catch their prey in midair. About 1,000 species live in North America.

BUG BYTES

Tabanid flies have been known to fly as fast as 90 miles per hour (145 km/h)!

Favorite Foods

A fly's **habitat** depends largely on what it eats. So, what do flies like to eat? We know that houseflies like many of the foods you enjoy, such as watermelon and hamburgers. But, flies do not eat these foods the same way you do.

Flies actually absorb the moisture from these foods. That is because flies can eat only liquid foods. So, they are especially attracted to rotting foods and garbage. Foods that are decaying become soft and release the moisture flies need.

Food must be soft or mushy before flies can lap it up with their

Chemicals in a housefly's saliva digest food outside its body. Similar chemicals help digest food inside your stomach.

spongelike labella. They even spit up **saliva** to turn solids into liquids. Then, they can suck the food into their strawlike mouths.

After a fly eats, food travels through the **digestive** system. First, the food enters the foregut. Then, food travels to the midgut. There, it is digested and absorbed. Finally, waste is released from the hindgut.

Blowflies are generally the first to arrive at a decaying body. They can detect the smell from more than 115 feet (35 m) away!

Garbage and rotting food are not the only gross foods flies like to eat. Their diet often includes animal waste and dead tissue. For example, blowflies lay their eggs on or in dead animals. When the eggs hatch, the larvae immediately begin to eat.

Other fly species live on true liquid food. Can you guess what it is? Blood! This is the main food of female mosquitoes, horseflies, and blackflies.

Female flies eat blood to develop their eggs. But most males do not eat blood.

These bloodsucking insects have needlelike mouthparts that pierce an animal's or a person's skin. They **inject saliva**, which keeps the blood from clotting. Then, strong pumps in their heads suck blood into their bodies.

Feeding on flowers is more common than feeding on blood. Adult flies visit a wide variety of flowers. They gather water, nectar, and pollen. Pollen is an important source of energy for flies that do not feed on blood.

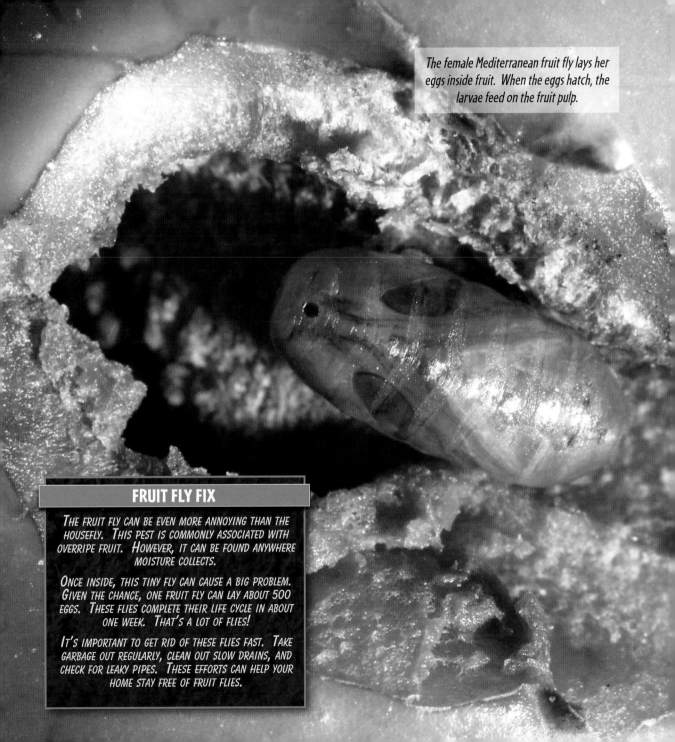

The female Mediterranean fruit fly lays her eggs inside fruit. When the eggs hatch, the larvae feed on the fruit pulp.

FRUIT FLY FIX

The fruit fly can be even more annoying than the housefly. This pest is commonly associated with overripe fruit. However, it can be found anywhere moisture collects.

Once inside, this tiny fly can cause a big problem. Given the chance, one fruit fly can lay about 500 eggs. These flies complete their life cycle in about one week. That's a lot of flies!

It's important to get rid of these flies fast. Take garbage out regularly, clean out slow drains, and check for leaky pipes. These efforts can help your home stay free of fruit flies.

Beware!

Like most insects, flies have many natural predators. These hunters must be sneaky and quick to catch adult flies. If the predators are lucky, they will find a bunch of maggots to eat. This is an easy, filling feast.

Who are these tricky predators? Frogs and lizards enjoy eating both larvae and adult flies. Birds and bats swoop down on a fly meal. And let's not forget the Venus flytrap. These carnivorous plants snap shut on the unsuspecting flies that land on their leaves.

What is a fly to do when danger approaches? Hide! Run! Zip away! Flies have numerous ways to stay alive. Some species resemble bees or other dangerous insects. This discourages predators from getting too close.

Adult flies use their many sensory features to avoid predators. The hairs on their bodies signal the approach of danger. And, they use their compound eyes to watch for enemies.

BUG BYTES

A housefly's wings can beat about 200 times per second. A midge's wings can beat up to 1,000 times per second!

Flies are an important part of many spiders' diets. They catch their prey in sticky webs.

Flies and You

Flies that feed on animal waste include blowflies and houseflies.

Most people find flies very annoying. It's disgusting to see one walking all over your hamburger. It itches when they leave their **saliva** on you, and it hurts when they bite. Even worse, it's gross to find one filled with your blood.

Unfortunately, flies can also be dangerous. Many flies carry disease. As flies feed on dead animals, garbage, and animal waste, they pick up **germs**. When they move to their next food source, they may transfer those germs. This causes the spread of deadly diseases such as malaria and cholera.

Flies that aren't bugging you or transmitting diseases have a couple of helpful functions. In nature, flies move from plant to

Sometimes, hospitals use fly maggots to clean up dead tissue and diseased wounds. This method can be much more effective than medication.

plant, **pollinating** them in the process. Flies also help rotting plants and dead animals decay. This limits waste and puts **nutrients** back in the soil.

At first glance, flies may seem like major pests. However, they do a lot of good in this world. Perhaps you will be less annoyed with them from now on. The next time a fly decides to eat your snack, simply say thank you. Then, shoo it away!

Glossary

digest - to break down food into substances small enough for the body to absorb. The process of digesting food is carried out by the digestive system.

entomologist - a scientist who studies insects.

fertilize - to make fertile. Something that is fertile is capable of growing or developing.

germ - a harmful organism, such as bacteria, that causes disease.

habitat - a place where a living thing is naturally found.

inject - to forcefully introduce a substance into something.

metamorphosis - the process of change in the form and habits of some animals during development from an immature stage to an adult stage.

nerve - one of the stringy bands of nervous tissue that carries signals from the brain to other organs.

nutrient - a substance found in food and used in the body to promote growth, maintenance, and repair.

organ - a part of an animal or a plant that is composed of several kinds of tissues and that performs a specific function. The heart, liver, gallbladder, and intestines are organs of an animal.

pheromone - a chemical substance produced by an animal. It serves as a signal to other individuals of the same species to engage in some kind of behavior.

pollinate - when birds and insects transfer pollen from one flower or plant to another.

saliva - a liquid produced by the body that keeps the mouth moist.

segment - any of the parts into which a thing is divided or naturally separates.

spine - a stiff, pointed projection on an animal.

How Do You Say That?

antennae - an-TEH-nee
chitin - KEYE-tuhn
cholera - KAH-luh-ruh
Diptera - DIHP-tuh-ruh
entomologist - ehn-tuh-MAH-luh-jihst
ganglia - GANG-glee-uh
halteres - HAWL-tihrz
hemolymph - HEE-muh-lihmf
labella - luh-BEH-luh
larvae - LAHR-vee
metamorphosis - meh-tuh-MAWR-fuh-suhs
ovipositor - OH-vuh-pah-zuh-tuhr
pheromone - FEHR-uh-mohn
proboscis - pruh-BAHS-kuhs
pupae - PYOO-pee
tracheae - TRAY-kee-ee

Web Sites

To learn more about flies, visit ABDO Publishing Company on the World Wide Web at **www.abdopublishing.com**. Web sites about flies are featured on our Book Links page. These links are routinely monitored and updated to provide the most current information available.

Index